What Would You Do?
A Child's Book About Divorce

by Barbara S. Cain, M.S.W. and Elissa P. Benedek, M.D.

Illustrated by James Cummins

Dedicated to the children who helped write this book.

Anna Csaky-Chase

YOUTH PUBLICATIONS/THE SATURDAY EVENING POST COMPANY

Copyright©1976 by The Saturday Evening Post Company, Indianapolis, Indiana. All rights reserved.

INTRODUCTION

We write this book for the children of divorce who must manage a host of feelings they cannot easily articulate or understand.

And too, we write for parents, themselves preoccupied, yet eager to help their children, eager to learn how divorce and its surrounding events impact upon their particular child.

Each child's reaction is, of course, uniquely his own. Nevertheless, we have observed through countless conversations with children a series of themes, a set of common reactions shared by many children as we see them in our schools, play groups, and clinics.

One by one, on each page of this book, we present these themes openly, directly, honestly. Together, they represent the child's experience, the child's story written by youngsters we have come to know during various phases of their parents' separation.

As this book asks the question "What would you do?" we invite the child to look within, to explore, express and eventually accept feelings he or she otherwise harbors alone.

As the book answers the question "What would you do?" we neither suggest nor recommend a "preferred" reaction. We simply present with candor what many children do, in fact feel, thereby showing the child these responses are normal, shared, and often transient.

No two children, even in the same family, will use this book precisely the same way. Indeed, it has been our experience that each child will vary its use during different stages of his or her parents' divorce. Typically, the youngster will select those themes that more nearly match his or her current concerns, selecting anew as new feelings emerge and re-emerge.

As we present these emotional issues in straightforward fashion, we encourage youngsters to take the lead, to express their thoughts and feelings with equal candor in the reassuring presence of a parent or friend.

It is our hope, then, that this text will inspire open and frank discussion between parent and child, student and teacher, brother and sister, and begin a process the children can use again and again as they come to terms with their parents' divorce and continue the business of growing up.

What if your Mom and Dad stopped talking together, and laughing together, and stopped being friends?

WHAT WOULD YOU DO?

I got a belly ache.

What if your Mom and Dad were hollering back and forth, and screaming back and forth, and you couldn't fall asleep?

WHAT WOULD YOU DO?

What if your Mom and Dad were so busy fighting they even forgot your birthday?

WHAT WOULD YOU DO?

I promised Thumper I'd never do that to her.

What if your Mom and Dad had their scariest fight the day you traded your sister for an all-day sucker?

WHAT WOULD YOU DO?

I started thinking it was all my fault.

What if you traded back the all-day sucker, but your Mom and Dad went on fighting anyway?

WHAT WOULD YOU DO?

I quit thinking it was all my fault.

I asked, "What's a divorce?"

What if your Mom and Dad told you they were getting unmarried—that your Dad would live in one house and your Mom in another?

WHAT WOULD YOU DO?

I wished there could be two of me.

I chose both.

What if you saw your Dad only on Sundays?

WHAT WOULD YOU DO?

I wished for a whole week of Sundays.

What if you were waiting for your Mom to come home from work, and it got darker, and later, and lonelier—but she still didn't come?

WHAT WOULD YOU DO?

I thought she went away just like my Daddy did.

I was wrong.

What if you had to move to a new house, and go to a new school, and make friends with kids who already had friends?

WHAT WOULD YOU DO?

I opened a lemonade stand and made four old cents and five new friends.

I said, "My Daddy's home is in a different house, and he gets to see me on Sundays."

What if you saw your Mom holding hands with a man you never even met?

WHAT WOULD YOU DO?

I got jealous.

I knew I had a Daddy on the days between Sundays.

What if you were lying in bed at night,
and there was no hollering back and forth,
and screaming back and forth—and that noise
in your head finally shut off?

WHAT WOULD YOU DO?

I fell asleep without even trying.

I knew I had a Mom. I knew I had a Dad.
I knew they both had ME!

Barbara S. Cain is a psychiatric social worker with clinical experience in residential treatment centers for children, child guidance clinics, and family service agencies serving both parents and children. She is a graduate of the University of Michigan and is currently with the University of Michigan's Student Mental Health Clinic.

Her clinical research and publications in both scientific journals and lay magazines focus upon problems of parent-child separation. Her articles include studies of the school phobic child, the impact of divorce on children, child loss, homesickness, and more recently, the empty-nest syndrome.

She lives in Ann Arbor, Michigan, with her husband and two sons.

Elissa P. Benedek is a child psychiatrist and the Training Director for the Center for Forensic Psychiatry in Ann Arbor, Michigan. Much of Dr. Benedek's work and writing has been in the area of divorce, exploring its impact on the children involved and examining relationships and feelings between parents and children. She is also active in child psychiatry panels, services, and committees.

Dr. Benedek's writings include articles in national psychiatry and medical journals. She reviews articles for the American Journal of Psychiatry and is a consultant to the Huron Valley Child Guidance Clinic. She received her training from the University of Michigan medical school.

Dr. Benedek lives in Ann Arbor, Michigan, with her husband and four children.

James Cummins attended Washington University School of Fine Arts. As a free-lance artist, he has illustrated children's textbooks and storybooks, as well as juvenile stories and articles, and has worked in many areas of religious publishing.

Cummins enjoys the variety and challenge of children's illustrations and feels that *What Would You Do* is a good example of this challenge.

He and his artist wife live in St. Louis, Missouri. They have two grown children.